ABT

E L

S K A

LOOP

A jump taking off
backward from an
outside edge
and landing in
a backward direction
on the same edge.

LUTZ

A jump taking off from a long glide backward
on the outside edge of one skate, with a
boost from behind from the other toe.
The backward landing is on the outside
edge of the opposite (boosting) skate.

SALCHOW

(sou cou)

A jump starting
from a back inside edge, landing
backward on the outside edge of the opposite skate.

CRESTWOOD HOUSE
Parsippany, New Jersey

For Robert Shaughnessy,
who loved books, too

Acknowledgments

I thank the following people for helping me to make this book:

Doug Leigh, and the Mariposa School of Skating.
Paul Harvath, Irene and Elvis Stojko, Barb McCutcheon, and Joanne McLeod.
Mary Lloyd at the Richmond Hill Public Library, and Elise Feeley and Elise Dennis at Forbes Library.
Barb Wilson and the Canadian Figure Skating Association.

James Chatto, Barbara McCutcheon, Sandra Martin, the CFSA, the *Toronto Star*, *American Skating World*, *Skating*, the *Winnipeg Free Press*, the *Ottawa Citizen*, the *Edmonton Journal*, *Châtelaine*, *The Sporting News* (Feb. 28, 1994 issue), the *Richmond Hill Liberal*, the *Richmond Hill Month*, Doug Leigh, and Elvis Stojko, for sharing their words.
McClelland & Stewart for quotes from *Figure Skating: A Celebration* by Beverley Smith. Edited by Dan Diamond. Distributed in the United States by St. Martin's Press.
Maclean's magazine: February 3, 1992; March 15, 1993; and March 20, 1995.
The New York Times for quotes on pages 9, 29-30, and 56. Copyright © 1994/95 by the New York Times Company. Reprint by permission.

Paul and Michelle Harvath, Stephan Potopnyk, Jean Bradshaw at the Toronto Star, and Dave Teetzel of the Richmond Hill Liberal for photographic assistance.
Writers Carol Weis, Nancy S. Carpenter, Elaine Streeter and Tom McCabe, the Hatfield group, Susan Aller, Ann Turner, Barbara Goldin, and Jane Yolen.
Skater and teacher Sarah Dickenson, and the gang at the Mullins Center.
Kids and teachers at the Jackson Street School.

My husband, Peter; Brian and Keely; Mom and Dad; and Eleanor. They have supported me in invaluable ways, the greatest of which is love.

Photo Credits

Front cover: Stephen Potopnyk.

Allsport/Shaun Botterill: 37. AP/Wide World Photos: 54. Canapress Photo Service: 7, 22, 23, 25, 28, 46, 47, 50, 55, 58. The Photographic Edge/Stephan Potopnyk: 4, 32, 44, 57. Courtesy, The Richmond Hill Liberal: 59. Linda Shaughnessy: 14. Toronto Star/K. Beaty: 40; T. Bock: 39; A. Dunlop: 17, 18; P. Gower: 10, 12; Mike Slaughter: 34. Glossary Illustrations: © 1998 David Uhl Studios; Ice Backgrounds © 1998 Bruce Bennet Studios

Library of Congress Cataloging-in-Publishing Data

Shaughnessy, Linda.
    Elvis Stojko: skating from the blade/by Linda Shaughnessy.—1st ed.
       p. cm.—(Figure skaters)
       Includes bibliographical references and index.

    Summary: A biography of the dynamic Canadian skater who successfully blended martial arts with figure skating to win the 1994 and 1995 World Championships.
       ISBN 0-382-39451-8.—ISBN 0-382-39452-6 (pbk.)
       1. Stojko, Elvis, 1972- —Juvenile literature.
    2. Skaters—Canada—Biography—Juvenile literature.
      [1. Stojko, Elvis, 1972-. 2. Ice skaters.] I. Title. II. Series.
GV850.S77S73 1998
796.332'092–dc20
[B]   96-25809

 Published by Crestwood House
A Division of Simon & Schuster
299 Jefferson Road, Parsippany, NJ 07054

First Edition
Printed in the United States of America
10 9 8 7 6 5 4 3 2 1

CONTENTS

Elvis's explosive power sends him airborn.

LEAPING WIZARD

*. . . it's not if you fall down that matters,
it's how fast you get up.*

• Elvis

The skater rose in the air, spinning, suspended like a held breath. He touched down on one foot, chips of ice flying from his blade, revealing the true force of landing. In less than two seconds, the **jump** was complete.

The music changed. He played with the beat, pushed and pulled it, danced it around. It was not ballet he was doing, but a new bag of movements—leaning, reaching, kicking. Power surged from his uncoiling knees to the tips of his fingers. He was skating from the blade.

The place was Red Deer, Alberta, Canada, in November 1994. The spectators at the Skate Canada competition were on their feet in praise of the young man who was 5 feet 7 inches tall and weighed 152 pounds. To the music from *1492:*

Conquest of Paradise, the story of Columbus, Elvis Stojko (STOI-koh) captured first place in their hearts, as well as with the judges. He bowed from the waist and opened his arms to them all.

It was one of his best skates, he said. He felt he was right on schedule in his training. Twenty-two years old, he was already Canadian national and world champion. In Halifax in January and in Birmingham, England, in March, he planned to defend those titles and bring home more gold medals to Richmond Hill, Ontario.

In the future the 1998 Olympics beckoned. He could become the first Canadian skater to win Olympic gold in men's singles.

But after landing a double **axel** jump in practice at the Canadian **Nationals** in Halifax in January 1995, his skate **edge** lost its grip on the ice. He careened into the corner, driving his right leg—his landing leg—into the wall that borders the ice, and wrenching the bones.

He tried to stand up and fell again. He had no feeling in his ankle. His promising season seemed over before it had begun.

The doctors said he had a tear in the ligament that holds the lower leg bones together, and the muscles were pulled. The next day he could hardly walk or pull his skate over his swollen foot. From ankle to knee, his leg hurt badly.

6

Two days later, people were shocked when Elvis skated onto the ice for his **short program** at the Nationals. He had already been assured of a place on the team going to the **World Championships**. What was he doing out there?

Elvis had been advised that competing would not aggravate his injury. Could he get through his program? Could he finish with a medal? He would wonder for the rest of his life if he didn't push himself to the limit and try.

Landing a triple axel, he fell, groaning in agony. His ankle collapsed again as he did some footwork. Elvis doubled over, right foot hanging, and shook his head. Gliding to the judges' table, wet-faced, he withdrew. It had been an excruciating 58 seconds for the 8,000 fans in the audience, too. Standing, they overflowed with support for his courage.

Pain glazed his deepset eyes. Painful, too, were questions about the future. The World Championships were only eight weeks away. Doctors doubted that he could recover in time.

This was his greatest challenge so far. What had he learned in his 22 years to prepare him for this?

Withdrawing from the short program, Elvis ends the audience's agony, but his own has just begun.

2

I WANNA DO THAT!

There are dreams I've had since I was little . . .
• Elvis

On March 22, 1972, Irene and Steve Stojko welcomed their third child into the world. They had already chosen his name, Elvis, after the King of rock 'n' roll, Elvis Presley. They had come to Canada in 1956, Steve from Slovenia and Irene from Hungary. They met, married, and started a landscaping business. Irene helped with the business while raising their daughter, Elizabeth, and son, Attila. Elizabeth and Attila were already teenagers when Elvis was born. Irene decided to stay home with Elvis on their farm near Newmarket, Ontario. "I knew I would have a boy, and I knew that he would be special," she said.

From the start, it looked as if she was right. Though it takes most babies a year to develop the balance and strength to walk, Elvis was toddling when he was only nine months old. At about age three, he walked by the television set and stopped. A figure skater was jumping and spinning on the screen.

"I wanna do that!" said Elvis. Skating looked like fun. He said it over and over until, when he was five, his mother finally took him to a rink in Newmarket. "They thought it was only a phase," Elvis said later. "It's been a long phase."

That first time on the ice, his mother watched him run and twirl, tumble and laugh. She signed him up for skating lessons. He and the other children followed the teacher like puppies, learning to balance and glide. Before long, Elvis was ready for serious figure skating lessons.

From the beginning, he especially loved jumping, spinning in the air. He learned to turn halfway around in the air in a **waltz jump**, and then all the way around in **toe loops**, **salchows** (sou-couz), **loops**, **lutzes**, and **flips**. Axels were harder—1 $\frac{1}{2}$ times around.

Elvis listened carefully to his teacher and to other adults. Then he thought things out and did them his own way. "Trust me, Mom." he'd say, "I know what I'm doing." His mother knew he wouldn't do reckless or crazy things. Elvis used his head.

One day, when he was almost seven, they went shopping. She remembers, "I fell in love with this little dirt bike, and I said, 'Elvis, would you like to have one?'" Of course, he said "Yes!"

Irene and Stephen Stojko help to anchor Elvis to what really matters: family, friends, and being himself.

Like Attila on his bigger bike, Elvis began riding around their farm with Prince, his German shepherd racing alongside. Balancing and leaning into turns felt a little like skating. The boy who loved jumping wasn't content to keep his wheels on the ground. He wanted to fly on his bike the way he did on his skates.

At the rink, summers and winters, many hours a day, Elvis did **spirals** and **camels**, **scratch spins** and **sit spins**. He threw himself into double jumps, spinning around twice before landing. He used his brain as well as his body and blades, thinking about the movements, and paying close attention to how they felt when he did them.

They didn't come easy to him. It took a lot of tries and a lot of falls to learn something new. "One more time," he'd say to his mother after a long day. It could be ten more until he did the jump or **spin** well enough to please himself.

"As a youngster, we couldn't get him off the ice," said his father. "And he just kept getting better." When Elvis was nine, they went to the Toronto Cricket Club to talk to well-known coach Ellen Burka.

3

SERIOUS

He always lands on his feet, whether he's soaring on the ice, jumping out of a tree, or rolling out of a fall on a dirt bike.
• Sean Rice to writer Sandra Martin

Ellen Burka watched little nine-year-old Elvis skate and decided to coach him.

"Mrs. Burka was a good teacher. She put him in the senior session when he was just a baby," said Mrs. Stojko. "She said, 'You just go in a corner and don't bother those big guys, but you skate with them.'"

Figure skating is both athletic and artistic. Mrs. Burka saw that Elvis loved jumping. "Learn the triples," was her plan for him; "it's of the utmost importance. The artistry you can learn later."

Skaters who dream of being world champions have to pass a series of tests. At each step there are moves to be mastered and competitions to enter. From novice to junior to senior, skaters

When Elvis was young, he learned from older skaters. Now the young ones look up to him.

climb the ladder to the Nationals, World Championships, and Olympics.

In competitions, Elvis learned to perform before audiences. Alone on the ice, he concentrated on what came next—which foot should he be on? Which edge? Was his arm creeping forward again? If he fell, he had to get up and go on, as if nothing had happened. The time to nurse bruises to his body or his pride was later.

Elvis first competed with skaters in the greater Toronto area. Then he and his mother traveled farther. Elvis was fierce competition. He did so well that his mother advised him not to let the standing ovations go to his head. He had noticed how some skaters had superior attitudes about their skills. It was hard for him to understand. His head and his heart didn't seem to work that way.

The people at the rink felt like family to him. At one competition he met Sean Rice, a **pairs skater**. Sean remembers Elvis as "a little short guy who could jump all over the ice." They became as close as brothers.

Irene would wake Elvis at 5:00 A.M., so he could be on the ice at 6:00 A.M. to practice. The chilly rink smelled like stale sweat and refrigeration. After a couple of hours, she would drive him to school. After school, he'd practice some more. He went to bed early, so he could do it again, day after day.

The cost of skates, time on the ice, coaching, costumes, and traveling to competitions was at least $10,000 a year. A pair of skating boots and blades could cost between $600 and $1000. They might last nine months, if he didn't outgrow them first. Fortunately the Stojko landscaping business was prosperous enough to pay for these costs. Elvis seemed to have a passion for figure skating. His parents quietly encouraged him and watched. And drove.

His father, Steve, had been a gymnast and soccer player in Slovenia. He thought Elvis should take up another sport besides skating. So when he was 10, Elvis stepped barefoot into the world of karate, the Japanese martial art.

He learned kicks, strikes, blocks, and other new ways to move his body. He sparred with students at the dojo, the karate school. There were drills to make him stronger and more flexible. There were ways of breathing to release power and clear his mind, so that he could listen to the voice inside him.

In the peace of the dojo, his spirit grew stronger, more patient, more persistent. Karate helped him at school and waiting to compete and picking himself up from a fall.

Richmond Hill, site of the largest optical telescope in Canada, and traversed by Yonge Street, the longest street in the world, has a new claim to fame—Elvis.

When Elvis came home from the dojo, he would show his father the new things he had learned. One day Steve stepped into Elvis's brand new hook kick. His broken ribs took no shine off the pride he felt for his son.

When the Stojkos moved to Richmond Hill, Elvis found areas near the house for dirt biking. He explored, getting to know the trails before riding full speed over them. Starting with little jumps, Elvis slowly built up to more amazing tricks, flying several feet in the air or plunging down steep slopes.

At age 13, though still small, Elvis had grown beyond the "big guys" at the Toronto Cricket Club. He was doing some triple jumps. He had placed third in the novice Canadian Nationals competition. Mrs. Burka and his parents thought that he needed new challenges and an advanced male skater to train beside.

The Canadian national champion, Brian Orser, trained in Orillia, a two-hour drive from Richmond Hill. All the young skaters were in awe of him. So it was all right with Elvis when he and his parents called on Doug Leigh, the man who was coaching Orser to excellence.

4

IN THE
SHADOWS

*When you love doing something,
the hard work doesn't seem so hard.*
• Elvis

At the Mariposa School of Skating, Elvis made new friends. Under the banner that read "You're in Triple Axel Country," there was much to learn. Elvis had a lot of questions.

"Excellent questions," Doug Leigh remembers, "and he was someone who listened." Elvis's eyes were glued to Leigh's face. In them the coach saw drive, will, heart—qualities he could nurture.

"Elvis always wore his own shoes," the coach said. The boy was his own person. He believed in himself. Leigh believed, too.

To allow time for training and traveling to competitions, Elvis attended a private high school. He endured teasing about his name, his size, and his figure skating. Some kids didn't like that he did things on his own and that he made his own decisions. Then the day came when he lifted a classmate by the throat and held him against a locker for a seemingly long time. The teasing stopped.

At 14, he was flying with double axel and triple lutz jumps and pushing hard to add more triples to his repertoire. As they shared practice time, Elvis admired Brian Orser's jumps and the way he expressed himself in his skating.

"Brian was there for me from the day Doug became my coach," Elvis says. "I learned so much from him—about training, attitude, how to handle interviews, how everything is done, and, most of all, that you're a person first and a skater second."

Nicknamed "Mr. Triple Axel," Orser was outjumping nearly everyone. In 1987 he landed six triple jumps, two of them triple axels, to become world champion. In 1988 he was the silver medalist at the Calgary Olympics. Soon after, he resigned his amateur status and turned professional.

Kurt Browning, another Canadian, took over from Orser. At the 1988 World Championships in Paris, he landed the first **quadruple jump** ever in competition, spinning around four times in eight tenths of a second.

Elvis kept an eye on those ahead of him, challenging himself to do what they could do, and more. With programs choreographed by Michelle Leigh, in 1988 he became the Canadian junior champion. Orser had been 17 and Browning 18 when they had reached that rung of the ladder. Elvis was only 15.

That same year Doug Leigh moved his skaters and coaches to the Allandale Recreation Centre, which he co-owned with the city of Barrie. They trained on two new rinks and off the ice—biking, running, lifting weights, doing aerobics and other conditioning. There were pools, a music library, places to live, and schools nearby. Skaters of all ages, from all over the world, could train seriously without sacrificing their education.

Elvis attended tutored and untutored classes at the high school next to the recreation center. When home, he raced and jumped with his bikes. At age 16 he earned his black belt in karate. He collected elfish blue Smurfs, got his driver's license, listened to music, and coped with the changes of a growing body.

These years were for shaping, strengthening, pushing the limits. "There's always a little more," his coach would say. "How far can we go?" Perhaps because of those body changes, as he was on the verge of adding a triple axel to his repertoire, Elvis's jumps went haywire. Finishing fifth in his divisional

The Canadian junior champion of 1988

Edges are everything. It would be hopeless and hazardous to perform in skates that weren't properly sharpened.

competition, he didn't qualify to go to the 1989 Nationals.

Kurt Browning became Canadian and world champion that year. His fame was suddenly enormous. But someone was skating all over his shadow.

As a result of months of relentless work to find his place in the air again, Elvis finished in first place in the next Divisionals.

The highlight of his performance was his first triple axel in competition. He rode the wave of his win to the 1990 National Championships.

A month later as he skated at the Nationals in Sudbury, Ontario, fans stood screaming so loudly that the volume of his music had to be turned up. Unable to hear himself think, 17-year-old Elvis finished a program that included eight triple jumps. Though the scores for his artistry showed room for improvement, in both the short and **long programs** Elvis received higher technical marks than Browning. There was astonishment and outcry when, overall, Browning won first place.

But second place meant that Elvis could skate for Canada at his first World Championships. Two months later, competing in Halifax, Nova Scotia, against the best in the world, he placed ninth. He was now one of the "skating elite."

According to *Figure Skating: A Celebration*, Elvis was later asked whether getting such a wild response from the audience that day in Sudbury made him feel powerful.

"No," he answered, without having to think. "It doesn't make me feel powerful. It makes me feel happy."

5

THE QUAD GOD

*I don't want skating to end up to be a ballet recital,
just a dance on ice or just another thing that girls
watch or people that are considered sophisticated . . .
It's a sport for everybody.*

• Elvis, to the *Winnipeg Free Press*

At the 1991 World Championships in Munich, Germany, onlookers got an unexpected show. While practicing, Kurt Browning and Elvis tried side-by-side quadruple jumps.

Kurt landed his jump better. So Elvis reeled off a quadruple toe loop/double toe loop **combination jump**. Then he did an arm-waving impersonation of Kurt's Hindu war god routine. Kurt joined him, jumping and playing me-and-my-shadow, while the crowd roared.

By now many skaters had landed quadruple jumps. Some had landed them in combination—the quad followed immediately by another jump. But no one had done this officially in a competition.

In his program at Munich, Elvis attempted the quadruple toe loop/double toe loop he had done in practice. He landed both jumps, making figure skating history. It was a sign of changes to come and his power to make them happen.

Does a quadruple jump feel "like being inside a washing machine during the spin cycle?" asked Laurie Nealin for the *Winnipeg Free Press*.

"If it does, you're in trouble," Elvis answered. "A jump, when it's done right, is very effortless and feels like you're floating. . . . If I had the energy, I'd be doing it all day."

Kurt Browning won the gold at Munich. Elvis came in sixth. He didn't mind hiding behind Kurt a while longer. Other skaters had to load their programs with difficult moves to keep up with him technically. But his artistic marks bothered him. He wanted to express who he was inside, but it wasn't coming out.

Ballet looks artistic. Elvis tried it. But ballet movements and frilly costumes weren't his style. He decided to work with something he understood and felt comfortable with—martial arts.

He learned kung fu, a Chinese martial art with circular movements similar to skating. His teacher, Glen Doyle, was impressed with Elvis's understanding of how his body worked. As Elvis learned new movements, he thought about them. His mind led his body, as it did when he was skating. When he didn't understand, he asked questions.

Elvis had another "teacher." Born in America of Chinese parents and reared in Hong Kong, Bruce Lee had studied

Third-place Paul Wylie applauds as Elvis wins Skate Canada in 1991.

kung fu. Returning to America in 1959, he taught kung fu not only to Asians but also to anyone who seriously wanted to learn. He developed his own discipline called Jeet Kune Do, the Way of the Intercepting Fist, which he displayed on television and in action movies, before his mysterious death in 1973.

Having seen Bruce Lee's movies, Elvis said, "He went against everything and proved that it worked."

Lee had studied psychology and philosophy to learn about himself. Following his example, Elvis enrolled part-time at York University. And he worked on programs for the upcoming season, including, he hoped, the Olympics in Albertville, France.

When Kurt Browning developed back spasms that kept him from competing at the 1992 Nationals in Moncton, Elvis was expected to win. But Michael Slipchuk, though hampered by nosebleeds, skated into first place. Elvis came in second, good enough to make the Olympic team.

Afterward the Stojko team revealed that because of a fractured bone in his foot, Elvis had not practiced his triples for nearly a month. He had used martial arts to handle the

pain and help him heal. It would not be the last time.

Elvis was an Olympian! In Albertville, France, the 19-year-old marched with his teammates in the opening parade and watched the flames of the torch leap to life.

After the short program he was sitting nicely in sixth place. In the freestyle program he held onto his landings while the rest of the men fell. But a seemingly impossible thing happened. Elvis dropped in the final standings to seventh place. They might as well have not watched him skate, it was said of the judges. Did they pass over Elvis because he was not expected to win?

Doug Leigh said, "We outskated them all! You think—Man, I got ripped. But you just eat it. You have no choice."

"I was very hurt at the marks," said Irene Stojko, clouding with anger, to writer James Chatto. "Everyone knows how beautifully he skated."

Elvis tried to accept the result. He couldn't change it. In the way of a martial artist, he took what was useful and positive from the experience. Then he let go of the rest and moved on.

Elvis flies through the air as he performs his freestyle program at the Olympics in Albertville, France.

23

6

INTO THE SPOTLIGHT

*The artistic side has to come from within . . . We had
to allow it to happen in a very natural, Elvis way.*
• Doug Leigh, to writer James Chatto

A month after Albertville, it was World Championships
time again. Elvis celebrated his twentieth birthday with his
mother and coach on the plane to Oakland, California.

If he had wished for a medal before blowing out his
candles, then his wish came true. On the podium next to
Viktor Petrenko and Kurt Browning, Elvis bent his head to
receive the bronze medal. It was a victory for him, and it
was the first time two Canadians had stood on the men's
singles podium.

From seventh to third place in a month? Things were
going faster than Doug Leigh had planned. Five days a week
Elvis trained from 7:00 A.M. until one in the afternoon, on
the ice and off.

"Some days I get bored with training," Elvis admitted to

Steadfast Elvis skates to a bronze medal at the
1992 World Championships in Oakland, California.

a writer for *Maclean's* magazine, "but that's when I'm not looking for new things to do. I have to set new goals all the time, higher and higher, better and better."

At an empty rink his new choreographer, German champion Uschi Keszler, told Elvis to "fool around to the music the way you do when you think nobody is looking." Instead of teaching him her way of skating, she studied his way, and together they fine-tuned it.

They designed a short program to powerful music from the movie *The Killing Fields*. Elvis chose another movie soundtrack, *Far and Away*, for a long program that included eight triple jumps and quad/double toe loop and triple lutz/triple loop combinations. In the autumn at Skate Canada, he won first place with them. The 1993 Nationals in Hamilton, Ontario, were next.

People had been talking about a showdown between Elvis and Kurt Browning since they had shared the podium in Oakland. It was good for the sport of skating. The Copps Coliseum in Hamilton sold out all 17,125 seats for the men's long program. Over two million people watched on television.

"I'm out of his shadow," said Elvis. To prove it, he skated with such excellence that he earned a perfect score of 6.0 for technical merit from one judge.

Nonetheless, Browning regained the gold while Elvis took the silver. But at the gala, the show after the competition, the crowd responded warmly to Elvis. His artistry was coming across.

Leigh matched the temperature and hardness of his ice to that in the rink in Prague, where the Worlds were soon to be held. Under the banner "You Are Now in Quadruple Country," Elvis ran through his programs until he could do them on autopilot, without thinking. "Now there is the possibility of finishing first," he said. "I can almost taste it."

Again the gold went to Browning and the silver to Elvis. Canada was proud.

Elvis had become a star. Teens screamed for him. Charities invited him to appear at benefits.

For a television special, *Elvis Airborne*, he was filmed dirt biking in the desert, doing martial arts, roller blading, skating, and spending time with his family. Stuntman and kung fu expert David "Stretch" Stevenson was hired to train Elvis for the biking and martial arts shots. Stevenson soon realized that his seemingly fearless student could already jump off mountains. They ended up teaching each other, as friends. Elvis designed his stunts and did them his own way.

It was time to add an agent to the "Stojko team" to plot a smart business course. The Stojko family had put thousands and thousands of dollars into Elvis's career. Now money was beginning to flow the other way. But to keep his status as an amateur, Elvis had to follow strict rules about earning money and spending it.

World Champion Kurt Browning and Elvis with his first World Silver Medal.

The Stojko house had become a beehive. Some mornings Irene found it hard to get dressed because of so many phone calls. At the kitchen table she and Elvis waded through fan mail, replying with a handwritten note or an autographed photo with a personal message. Sometimes, he'd escape to the garage, flick on the radio to a hip-hop music station, and tinker with the dirt bikes he had built with his Dad. He'd go for rides, leaving his dog, Prince, waiting, too old to keep up.

In his apartment in the basement of the house, amid exercise and audio equipment, Smurfs, stuffed animals from his fans, Samurai swords, and his medals, Elvis organized his life so he could have time for everything. He was rarely at home. And now he was in demand for ice shows.

That spring Elvis joined a ten-city Stars on Ice tour. By watching the polished performers, he became one of them. Canadian skater and artist Toller Cranston noticed that Elvis "discovered something that people will tell you, but that you don't really believe—to concentrate on what you do best. So while I skated in black velvet and white satin, he would skate in jeans and a T-shirt."

Practicing **backflips** one day, Elvis's legs didn't make it over his head. His face slammed into the ice. "I'm lucky I didn't break my neck," Elvis told *The New York Times*. "I had blood all over my face and I couldn't see. The skin had fallen over my eye. . . . It was open all the way to the bone." He had it stitched up, and the next day he went out and did another backflip. "I had to . . . but I haven't tried one since."

The upcoming season included the Olympic games at Lillehammer, Norway. After seeing the movie *Dragon: The Bruce Lee Story*, Elvis played the soundtrack for Uschi Keszler. "It's the biography of Bruce Lee, the way he lived, overcoming his inner beast," he said. "The music from his story is perfect for what I want . . . to get across who I am."

Kung fu movements imitate animals like the praying mantis, the tiger, and the crane. Elvis and "Stretch" Stevenson blended these moves with traditional skating elements.

While Elvis practiced, his mother designed and created a simple outfit, black with golden Chinese-style buttons and a sash to flow in his breeze. For his short program, to hip-hop music from *Frogs In Space*, he and his mother chose black leather. Irene attached over one hundred chrome grommets to the legs and shirt.

Finally, all was ready. Like Bruce Lee, he was making his own style, going against everything to prove that it works. But what would the judges say?

"I have to do my best for myself," said Elvis. "I'm the skater. Let the judges judge."

7

LILLEHAMMER

*. . . have a goal and go for it 100 percent and
don't let anyone change your mind.*

• Elvis

The top three men at the 1994 Canadian Nationals in Edmonton
would make the team to go to Lillehammer, Norway. Browning
had troubles. Though Elvis fell attempting a quad, his *Dragon*
program with eight triples won him the gold medal. After four
years of coming in second, at last he stepped up to the top tier of
the podium.

His father, Steve, said, "I just want to cherish this for the rest of
my life. I am so proud of this young man."

Elvis chose the gala after Nationals to unveil a surprise for his
parents. In a leather jacket exactly like the one the other Elvis
wore, he gyrated and bopped to "Jailhouse Rock" and "I Can't
Help Falling in Love With You." It was a playful side of Elvis that
few had seen.

The Sporting News saw Elvis in Lillehammer as "a Canadian

Elvis shows his playful side in a tribute to Elvis Presley.

kung-fu fighter wearing studs and leather, a rebel likely doomed to fail by the figure skating establishment before he takes the ice."

But most of the buzz was about Nancy Kerrigan. Her leg had been bashed by an attacker linked to Tonya Harding, who was also competing for the gold.

The International Skating Union also stirred up talk by allowing professional skaters to return and compete as amateurs. Champions Brian Boitano and Viktor Petrenko were taking advantage of the decision. To Elvis, it didn't seem fair, but those were the rules. He figured he'd finish fourth behind Boitano, Petrenko, and Browning.

Irene and Steve came to Norway to see their 21-year-old son skate, bringing the Richmond Hill flag to the ice arena. When the folks at home saw the flag on television, they cheered.

How did Elvis feel before competing? "Your legs feel funny, your system goes funny, things run through your mind, your confidence is tested," he said. But nerves and pressure generated energy that he channeled into his performance.

He knew he was consistent but not perfect. Anyone could have a bad day. He tried to relax and enjoy the entire Olympic experience. As determined as he was to skate his best there, he knew there would be other chances.

The night of the short program, Elvis took over the ice in his leather and chrome. Millions of viewers throughout the world got their first look at figure skating Stojko style. Dramatic Philippe Candeloro, skating for France, was another eye-opener, with his trademark squatting hops and ankle spins to music from *The Godfather*.

Russian Alexei Urmanov had a more traditional short program. Though his marks for required elements were lower than Elvis's, Urmanov ended in first place because of his high artistic scores. Elvis came in second, Candeloro came in third, and all three were well ahead of veterans Petrenko, Boitano, and Browning.

Some viewers questioned the judging. Paul Wylie, the 1992 Olympic silver medalist, told *The Sporting News*, "They don't like Elvis's style. He doesn't point his toes. He doesn't stretch in his camel spins. I mean, there are certain things he doesn't do that Urmanov does. But to me, he was actually interpreting his program . . . and it comes from the heart."

On the night of the freestyle skate, commentator Dick Button, former world and Olympic champion, explained the judging criteria: first the triples, then the overall impact of the program, followed by footwork, spins, and musicality.

What about quads? Urmanov had landed one at the 1992

As Bruce Lee on blades, Elvis makes martial arts an Olympic event.

Olympics. Would Elvis go for a quad or quad combination?

Waiting for his turn to skate, Elvis focused his thoughts. He needed to stay relaxed and let himself flow. Landing a quad, the triple would follow. He planned to go all out. What did he have to lose?

Petrenko, Browning, and Boitano pulled themselves up in the standings with strong performances. Candeloro skated smoothly to a longer piece from *The Godfather* but fell near the end on a triple axel.

Enter Elvis, wary, coiling, pushing out wide circles, pivoting in tight ones. He exploded into the air like fireworks and glided like ripples on a pond.

The time came for a quad combination. It didn't feel right. He flowed on, gathering energy. Then he unleashed a surprise triple axel/triple toe loop combination. As the last chord faded, he raised one hand toward the heavens, awaiting his fate.

His technical scores were two 5.8s and seven 5.9s. But his artistic marks hurt—5.6s to 5.8s and a 5.5 from the Russian judge. The spectators booed.

Urmanov landed eight triples and a combination. Elvis's technical marks again were higher. But after the artistic marks and technical marks were combined, Urmanov ranked highest with five of the judges and Elvis with the remaining four. The willowy Russian won the Olympic gold medal, Elvis took the silver, and Candeloro, the bronze.

He would let nothing stop him, Elvis had said. But he would not change himself to please the judges. He and Candeloro had shown them that quality skating comes in different costumes and styles. They were opening the door for younger skaters to do their own things.

Some of those younger skaters and Mayor Bill Bell were among the 1,700 fans in Richmond Hill who celebrated the homecoming of their local hero at the Observatory Arena. They presented Elvis with gifts, including an honorary life-time membership in the Richmond Hill Figure Skating Club. He autographed photos, flags, skates, money, and shirts and posed for pictures.

It was hard for Elvis to put words to what he was feeling. To these people he was already the king of figure skating. In a couple of weeks, he would board a plane to Japan for the next big event, the World Championships. As he signed and posed and answered questions, he gave each fan his full attention. It was his way. He would focus on skating when the time came, and he would be ready.

Elvis waves to fans after winning the Olympic silver medal.

8

"Air Stojko"

Figure skating is not like a best-of-seven series . . .
We're always playing sudden death and in sudden
death anything can happen.

• D o u g   L e i g h

Irene Stojko sat among the crowd of 5,000 spectators at the 1994 World Championships in Chiba, Japan. Her husband led the supporters back in Richmond Hill. As usual, it all came down to the freestyle program. It was March 23, the day after Elvis's twenty-second birthday. What had he wished for on the candles this time?

Alexei Urmanov attempted a quad and fell, but his countryman Viacheslav Zagorodniuk jumped with grace and ease. Philippe Candeloro challenged them with what some called the best performance of his career.

Skating his *Dragon* program for the last time in major competition, Elvis reeled off a quadruple toe loop, a beauty. Instead of following it with a double toe loop as planned, he went for the record for the first official quadruple/triple combination. So close! Unable to hold onto the landing, Elvis put a foot down.

When he came off the ice, awaiting his marks, he knew he had done his best, risen to his own challenge. Perfection was impossible. He had aimed for excellence.

As his technical scores were displayed above them, Doug Leigh cried out, "A six!" Elvis's eyes opened wide. Happy surprise washed over his face. Then his artistic marks came up, with four 5.9s among them.

Zagorodniuk took the bronze, Candeloro the silver. The new king, Elvis Stojko, was in the center with the gold medal around his neck, singing as the flag slowly rose, "Oh, Canada. . . ."

Back in Richmond Hill, the mayor invited Elvis to a little parade in his honor at noon on the Saturday before Easter. Starting at Roselawn Public School, for the next hour Elvis's black Sonoma vehicle was mobbed by fans. When the parade

On his return from Chiba, Elvis shows his father what he earned this time.

39

A new name for the local arena. The mayor says they'll hold off renaming the city until after Elvis wins the 1998 Olympics.

halted, he saw that Observatory Arena had a new name—Elvis Stojko Arena.

"I'm shocked," he said. "Thank you is not enough for what I feel inside me." He basked in the recognition for what he had accomplished with all his hard work. He knew it didn't make him better than anybody else—just happy.

The *Richmond Hill Month* reported, "Stojko is a polite young man with his head screwed on right . . . He's that all-important cool, yet kids can look at him and see how channeling your energy into something positive can really pay off."

The *Month* thanked Elvis: "If you never lace up another skate, you have put Richmond Hill on the map."

9

LONG LIVE THE KING

The music draws things out of you, and it feels great.
Even if I'm really tired, my body reacts
to it automatically.

• Elvis

It was time for the Campbell's Soups Tour of World Figure Skating Champions. In cities across the United States, Elvis shared the spotlight with Brian Boitano, Nancy Kerrigan, Viktor Petrenko, Oksana Baiul, and many other skating greats. Though he was a new champion, he got as much applause as the others when he appeared.

From April until July, he rode on a bus, rehearsed, ate, performed, and rode on a bus again. He slept when he could. How different this schedule was from a training schedule geared toward making him healthy and strong. It was a grind, but there were benefits.

Traveling together, skaters got to know one another and learned from one another. Elvis tried out new moves and played with the audience. And it was a relief having tour security people to protect his privacy. At home it was a different matter.

Most people were great and did not intrude on his personal life. But some thought nothing of interrupting him at a restaurant or movie.

Never much of a party goer, Elvis liked to do things at home. He invited in friends, played video games, or painstakingly put together model cars. His mother kept the refrigerator full of the foods he liked—milk, fruits, and vegetables. And ice cream. He says he feels better when he eats good food. "I'm really sensitive to that, to the way my body reacts to different things."

As long as he could get away from it once in a while, it wasn't a job; it was fun. His agent kept it that way, running interference, screening demands. From the many requests to put Elvis's name on this product or that, they chose Nokia, maker of the cellular phone Elvis used, and Gold Seal salmon.

Elvis told *Winnipeg Free Press* reporter Laurie Nealin about a 16-year-old girl who knew him and had skated with him. She was dying of cancer and wanted to see him. When he got to the hospital, she had just passed away, but she had known he was coming. "I didn't want to intrude, but her parents were very happy that I came," said Elvis. "I'm not usually one to cry much . . . but that day . . . I shed a few tears. I didn't realize how much of an impact I had on an individual."

He became the Kids' Ambassador to Ronald McDonald

Children's Charities of Canada, spending time with children with life-threatening illnesses and disabilities. Maureen Kitt of the Children's Charities told *International Figure Skating* magazine that Elvis was "warm, caring, and extraordinarily sensitive with all these children . . . they really felt that Elvis understood their daily challenges."

"Everyone has a mountain to climb," said Elvis. "As long as we're there to help each other . . . that's the basis of mankind."

He was learning a lot about life and about himself. On days off while touring and through the summer, he and Uschi Keszler worked on something different for next season. Martial arts were only a part of what was inside him. He worked on a new combination jump and chose music from the movies *Total Recall* and *1492: Conquest of Paradise*, the story of Columbus. It fit his own journey of self-discovery better than he could have imagined.

In September, when most amateurs settled down to heavy training, Elvis went on tour again. It was his own eight-city Canadian tour of champions, choreographed by Uschi Keszler. A dollar from each ticket sold would go to Ronald McDonald Children's Charities. There were performances by Philippe Candeloro, Surya Bonaly, **ice dancers** Shae-Lynn Bourne and Victor Kraatz, and many others. The highlights were filmed for a television special, *Elvis and Friends*.

Elvis's short program at the 1995 Canadian Nationals was cut shorter by the agony of his injured ankle.

Being in charge of it all was stressful. But the tour was so successful that Elvis decided to expand to ten cities when he did it again the next year.

That November Elvis tried out his new programs at Skate Canada in Red Deer, Alberta, and won the gold. In December he was voted Canadian Male Athlete of the Year, the Lyle Conacher Award, by Canadian sportswriters and broadcasters. Olympic gold medal skier Jean-Luc Brassard and hockey great Wayne Gretzky were a distant second and third. The Canadian Sport Council also chose Elvis for Athlete of the Year.

For the 22-year-old, 1994 had been quite a year—an Olympic silver, World gold, successful tours, and athlete of the year. But his freak fall and crash into the boards put an agonizing twist on what was to come.

10

THE TERMINATOR

*He's gone over hurdles, climbed over mountains,
dropped into valleys, and climbed out of them.
That's why they call him The Terminator.*

• Sean Rice, to writer Barb McCutcheon

The damage to his ligaments was so bad that some said it would have been better if the ankle had broken. From the night of his painful short program at Nationals to the opening of the World Championships in Birmingham, England, he had eight weeks to heal.

"Right off the bat, we took five days off," said Doug Leigh. "Then when we tried to put the skate on, it wouldn't fit."

Glen Doyle phoned Elvis in Halifax. He taught Elvis breathing and focusing exercises that would start the healing and control the pain. When Elvis got home, Doyle loosened and stretched the injured muscles without damaging them.

Elvis started having acupuncture, a technique of Eastern medicine, before and after training. He believed that it unblocked the flow of natural healing energy in his body.

The day after the injury, Elvis explains what happened.

"We used everything that was positive and real," said Leigh. "We never thought it couldn't be done." Like Columbus, in his long program Elvis was sailing uncharted waters. Day by day, coach and skater felt their way through the training. When triple and even double jumps were impossible, they went back to singles. The pain was intense.

Outwardly confident about recovering in time, Elvis, inside, rode an emotional rollercoaster of anger, disappointment, frustration, and doubt. The steps forward were little ones. "Trust me, Mum," he had always said. Now he had to trust himself to know when to push his ankle and how hard.

Testing, how hard can he push it, how much can it take?

He took time out to do a martial-arts demonstration with Glen Doyle. Doyle told the young students that Elvis's kicks would be low power because of his injury. Moments

47

later, with one of those kicks, Elvis lifted a fully padded Doyle off the floor.

In late February Elvis needed to see if the ankle would take triple jumps. "We got to the point, if it's gonna break, then it might as well break," said Leigh. "We reached that wall."

Landing a triple jump exerted tremendous force on his ankle, about 400 pounds. But that was not the worst for Elvis. Taking off from that ankle put torque on it, a forceful twist that shot pain right up his leg. But he refused to change the program, to substitute moves that would be easier on his ankle.

"Never turn back," said Leigh. "We're the ones who upgraded the elements. We want to force the hands of the other guys."

Elvis tried a triple axel and injured his knee. But a week later he could do every jump except the quad. They had gone through that wall.

Before the Stojko team departed for England, Leigh sat down with Elvis. "We can't train the way we want to this time. But your body has trained before," he said. "It knows, it's in place, mentally and physically. It knows where the autopilot button is." Elvis just had to trust it.

11

BIRMINGHAM

We don't do it because we have to,
we do it because we can.
• Doug Leigh

It was said to be the strongest field of men ever to compete for a medal. Russians Ilya Kulik and Alexei Urmanov were favored to win the gold, according to the Associated Press. U.S. champion Todd Eldredge's chances were "Excellent." Elvis was ranked "Fair."

Never one to worry about his competitors, Elvis focused all his energies on what he had to do. When he doubled over with pain from a fall in practice, onlookers were shocked. But he'd been dealing with pain all along. He continued acupuncture, martial-arts techniques, and physiotherapy. His mother was there with him. His roommate was his fellow teammate and long-time buddy Sean Rice.

On the evening of the short program, Elvis stormed the ice with high kicks and jumps. The fans forgot to hold their breath

Elvis, flanked by his choreographer Uschi Keszler and his coach Doug Leigh, gives a thumbs up as he gets his marks for the technical program.

about his ankle. There was no sign of trouble. Folks back home were thrilled but not surprised to see that Elvis was playing to win.

Todd Eldredge, also rebounding from injury and illness, earned towering marks for his jazzy short performance. He was first going into the freestyle program the next night followed by Stojko, Davis, Urmanov, and Candeloro.

They looked tough warming up. There was gangster Scott Davis, Godfather Candeloro, and Eldredge in Civil War blue and gray. Elvis wore a marine blue vest and white shirt that laced crisscross up the deep neck. At his throat a pendant, a gift from his aunt and uncle after Albertville, reflected sparks of light like a gold doubloon.

They skated tough warming up, outdoing one another with triple jumps. Elvis tried a quad, and landed it. Then the ice was cleared. His wait began.

Skating after Urmanov, first-place Eldredge looked eager. Although he doubled the second half of a triple axel/triple toe loop, he went on boldly. Landing his second triple axel, he fell; but with seconds left, he whipped out another one. The crowd erupted. His mother fell off the edge of her seat.

The French coach noted that Eldredge should have been penalized for attempting the same jump three times. Instead, the judges rewarded him. Todd's high marks left little room for anyone else to beat him.

"Backstage," Elvis smiled at the roving TV camera. He looked as if he were headed for an afternoon picnic, not the challenge of his lifetime. After Candeloro and Davis skated, it was his turn at last.

He glided over to Doug and Uschi. "At that moment, we'd worked hard, done everything we possibly could," said Leigh. "He just looked at me and said, 'We're doing this one for us. Whatever happens . . . !' "

Elvis shook Leigh's hand and skated off alone. At one end of the rink, perfectly still, he crouched like Columbus touching the sand after a harrowing voyage. The sound of waves grew loud. On the first beat of music, Elvis sprang.

He led with a triple flip. After a smooth triple/triple combination, his next jump, a triple loop, was wobbly but good.

He had planned an opportunity for a quad. No one else had done one, so he didn't have to. But could he? He went for it. After four perfect rotations, he landed—but touched his hand and other foot down to keep from falling.

After scissorlike footwork, with the fans clapping to the beat, Elvis leaped into a triple axel, followed by a triple lutz. Mouth open, he appeared to be gasping for air. With seconds left, there was one more triple planned, in combination with a double. Did he have the energy?

He rose into the first jump, touched down, and the crowd gasped. He soared into the air again for not two but three rotations. Elvis had thrown in an extra triple of his own!

Irene Stojko stood and whistled. Uschi Keszler jumped up and down. Doug Leigh looked for someone's hand to clap.

A spinning blur, Elvis came back into focus, stopped sharply, and raised his fists in the air. The fans in the exhibition center went berserk.

Elvis stepped off the ice and pulled his coach and golden-haired choreographer close, their three heads together for a private moment. Then the microphones moved in.

His marks were posted, including a perfect technical 6.0 from the French judge. The tally was quickly done. Elvis scored highest with six of the judges, Eldredge with three. Elvis was king again.

To a throng of reporters, Elvis explained how, after the quad, he had begun storing up the energy he needed for the extra triple. The gold medal meant even more to him the second time. He had worked so hard and come back against such strong skaters. "I trusted myself. I knew I could do it, and I proved that to myself," he said.

Elvis was feeling great. When Steve Stojko phoned the next day, Sean Rice reported that his roommate was at the rink, signing autographs. Elvis did a dazzling number at the exhibition after the competition. Despite the obvious waves of pain crossing his face, the crowd demanded an encore. Elvis strode out again with more fancy footwork and a smile.

Both having ended their programs with something extra, Elvis and Todd Eldredge take the top medals.

"There have been a lot of good skaters," Canadian coach David Dore told *The New York Times*, "but there have not been many with that kind of guts."

"Trying the quad was such a risk," said Uschi Keszler to a *Maclean's* reporter. "If he'd landed that the wrong way, he would have been out of there. But the only way Elvis knows how to compete is to go for broke."

"Last year he won the World Championships," said Doug Leigh. "This year he conquered the world."

The 1995 world champion soars at the exhibition after the competition.

12

WORLD CONQUEROR

*The next generation of
skaters may need a pilot's license.*

• James Deacon, *MacLean's* magazine

Air Stojko. Leaping Wizard. The Quad God. The Terminator. After conquering the world, what's next? Quadruple axels? With better equipment, jumps with five rotations? "There is always a little more," Doug Leigh says.

In 1995, Elvis was one of five Canadians chosen for the Meritorious Service Award for bringing honor to the country. On tours, when the spotlights flashed over him, the applause was riotous. How easy it would have been to get a swelled head.

But he says, "I've always tried to keep in contact with myself, Elvis Stojko the person, the guy that rides dirt bikes, the guy that does martial arts. That's what keeps me *me*, and I'll never change."

It's a balance he makes sure he maintains. His family and friends are at the center. He knows that they love him for

Elvis entertains spectators at a benefit show, Dreams on Ice.

Elvis hams it up during a visit to the Motorcycle Museum near Birmingham, England.

who he is, not for what he does.

In 1996, Elvis reclaimed his national title but lost his world title with a freak fall in his short program. The next season he came back stronger, sealing his win at the 1997 Nationals with a rare quad/double combination.

The first Olympic gold medal for Canada in men's singles was waiting to be won. After the 1998 Olympic games in Japan, Elvis may follow other dreams, perhaps competitive motocross racing or acting in action movies or teaching young athletes to "skate from the blade."

"No matter what you choose or what you do, always believe that you can," said Elvis, "because there's always a way of doing things, of getting through a problem. It's always a matter of how you look at it."

Even as a small boy waiting years for his first spin on the ice, Elvis had known. There's always a way.

Elvis and Doug Leigh's four-year-old son know that fun is what it's all about.

GLOSSARY

axel

A jump with a forward take-off on the outside edge of one skate, rotation(s), and an extra half-turn to land on the back outside edge of the opposite skate.

backflip

A gymnastic move from a backward glide, flipping the legs up and back over the head and landing on one or two feet.

camel

A one-foot spin with the body and other leg in a horizontal position.

combination jump

One jump followed by another, with no steps or turns between.

edge

The sharp inside or outside rim of the blade of a skate.

flip

A jump from the back inside edge of the skate, boosted by the toe of the other foot from behind. After rotating, the landing is on the back outside edge of the other skate (the boosting foot).

ice dancer

A skater who, with a partner, performs routines requiring dance elements, almost constant contact, and no lifts above the waist.

jump

Any of the various ways of leaping into a spin in the air and landing. The turns can be single, double, triple, or quadruple.

long program

The second part of a competition, also called the freestyle program, lasting 4 or 4 $\frac{1}{2}$ minutes and showing the skater's best skills and artistry.

loop

A jump taking off backward from an outside edge and landing in a backward direction on the same edge.

lutz

A jump taking off from a long glide backward on the outside edge of one skate, with a boost from behind from the other toe. The backward landing is on the outside edge of the opposite (boosting) skate.

Nationals

The yearly competition held in January or February to determine the champions who will represent a country at the World Championships and Olympics.

pairs skater

One of two partners skating in harmony and performing routines, including spins, jumps, high lifts, and throws.

quadruple jump, quad

A jump with a spin of 4 rotations, or 4 ½ for a quad axel.

salchow (SOU COU)

A jump starting from a back inside edge, landing backward on the outside edge of the opposite skate.

scratch spin

A very fast one-foot spin with legs and arms held close to the body.

short program

The first part of a competition, also called the technical program, lasting 2 minutes or 2 minutes and 40 seconds, including required moves such as 3 jumps, 3 spins, and 2 sequences of footwork.

sit spin

A one-foot spin in a sitting position.

spin

A twirling movement in a variety of positions, on either foot or both feet.

spiral

A one foot glide, forward or backward, with the other leg extended back straight and upward.

toe loop

A loop jump, assisted by a boost from behind from the other toe.

waltz jump

Taking off forward from an outside edge, turning halfway around and landing backward on the outside edge of the opposite foot.

World Championships

Competition between national champions to determine the best skaters in the world, usually held in March.

COMPETITION RESULTS

Year	Competition	Result
1988	Canadian Nationals (junior)	1st
1989	World Junior Championships	6th
1990	Canadian Nationals	2nd
	World Junior Championships	8th
	World Championships	9th
1991	Canadian Nationals	2nd
	World Championships	6th
	Skate Canada	1st
1992	Canadian Nationals	2nd
	Olympic Winter Games	7th
	World Championships	3rd
	Skate Canada	1st
1993	Canadian Nationals	2nd
	World Championships	2nd
1994	Canadian Nationals	1st
	Olympic Winter Games	2nd
	World Championships	1st
	Skate Canada	1st
1995	World Championships	1st
	Trophee Lalique	3rd
	NHK Trophy*	1st
1996	Canadian Nationals	1st
	Champion Series Final	2nd
	World Championships	4th
	Skate Canada	1st
	NHK Trophy*	1st
1997	Canadian Nationals	1st

*Given by the Japanese National
Government Broadcasting Corp.

For Further Reading

About Skaters

Browning, Kurt, and Neil Stevens. **Kurt: Forcing the Edge**. Toronto: Harper Collins, 1991.

Burakoff, Alexis. **On the Ice**. Newton, MA: Hare & Hatter Books, 1994.

Donahue, Shiobhan. **Kristi Yamaguchi: Artist on Ice**. Minneapolis: Lerner, 1993.

Faulkner, Margaret. **I Skate!** Boston: Little Brown, 1979.

Gordeeva, Ekaterina, and E.M. Swift. **My Sergei: A Love Story**. New York: Warner Books, 1996.

Hilgers, Laura. **Great Skates**. Boston: Little Brown, 1991.

Orser, Brian, and Steve Milton. **Orser: A Skater's Life**. Toronto: Key Porter Books, 1988.

Sanford, William, and Carl Green. **Dorothy Hamill**. Parsippany, NJ: Crestwood House, 1993.

Savage, Jeff. **Kristi Yamaguchi: Pure Gold**. New York: Dillon Press, 1993.

Shaughnessy, Linda. **Michelle Kwan: Skating Like the Wind**. Parsippany, NJ: Silver Burdett Press, 1998.

_____. **Oksana Baiul: Rhapsody on Ice**. Parsippany, NJ: Silver Burdett Press, 1998.

_____. **Scott Hamilton: Fireworks on Ice**. Parsippany, NJ: Silver Burdett Press, 1998.

About Skating

Indiana-World Skating Academy. **Figure Skating: Sharpen Your Skills**. Indianapolis: Masters Press, 1995.

Milton, Steve. **Skate: 100 Years of Figure Skating**. Toronto: Key Porter Books, 1996.

Sheffield, Robert, and Richard Woodward. **The Ice Skating Book**. New York: Universe Books, 1980.

Smith, Beverley. **Figure Skating: A Celebration**. Toronto: McClelland & Stewart, 1994.

Van Steenwyk, Elizabeth. **Illustrated Skating Dictionary for Young People**. New York: Harvey House, 1979.

Stories About Skating

Dodge, Mary M. **Hans Brinker or the Silver Skates**. Sisters, OR.: Questar, 1993.

Lowell, Melissa. Silver Blades series: **Breaking the Ice** (1993); **Competition** (1994); **Going for the Gold** (1994); **In the Spotlight** (1993). New York: Bantam.

Streatfeild, Noel. **Skating Shoes**. New York: Dell, 1982.

INDEX